I0147318

James Thompson

A Short Authentic Account of the Expedition Against Quebec in the Year 1759,

under command of Major-General James Wolfe. By a colunteer upon that

expedition.

James Thompson

A Short Authentic Account of the Expedition Against Quebec in the Year 1759, *under command of Major-General James Wolfe. By a colunteer upon that expedition.*

ISBN/EAN: 9783337321840

Printed in Europe, USA, Canada, Australia, Japan

Cover: Foto ©Andreas Hilbeck / pixelio.de

More available books at **www.hansebooks.com**

A SHORT AUTHENTIC ACCOUNT

OF THE

EXPEDITION AGAINST QUEBEC

IN THE YEAR 1759,

UNDER COMMAND OF MAJOR-GENERAL JAMES WOLFE.

BY A VOLUNTEER UPON THAT EXPEDITION.

Quebec:

PRINTED BY MIDDLETON & DAWSON, AT THE "GAZETTE"
PRINTING AND PUBLISHING ESTABLISHMENT.

1872.

NOTE.

The manuscript of the annexed narrative was circulated for half a century in Quebec by the late Deputy-Commissary-General Thompson, with a note to the effect that it was transcribed by him "from rough memoranda." From the high position which both he and his father had held in public estimation, for nearly a century, it was generally known as the "Thompson Manuscript." A short time before the removal of the Royal Engineers from Quebec, Mr. C. Walkem, an *employé* of the Department, in assorting the office-papers, discovered a manuscript, and, not being aware of the existence of the "Thompson Narrative," believed that it was an original document. Under this impression he shewed it to me, when I at once pronounced it a nearly *verbatim-et-literatim* copy of Thompson, and produced to him the original, which I left for some time in his possession. Mr. Walkem dissented from my view of the case, and in December last the manuscript found by him appeared in the *Canadian Illustrated News* as an original paper never before published, and being the production of a Major Moncrief, an Engineer of the Expedition. I at once took exception to this, which led to a lengthy correspondence, in the course of which it came out that the manuscript had been published among the Royal Engineer Corps papers in 1848, having been furnished by the late General Lewis, and that the copy found by Mr. Walkem was not, as he had alleged, a copy of the original of Major Moncrief, but had been transcribed by Mr. Pilkington, in 1857, by direction of Colonel Gallwey, from the Engineer Corps papers, for the information of Sir Wm. Eyre. Mr. Tregellas has since laid claim to the authorship for Major McKellar, the Engineer-in-Chief of the Expedition, but admits that they are not in possession of the original manuscript, which they have hitherto failed to discover. In the course of the controversy, among other statements it was alleged that the Moncrief manuscript was written in "the old style of the English of the year 1759, whereas the Thompson journal is written in the modern style." Mr. Charles Walkem has also written : " Strictly speaking, *there is nothing clear or well-defined* about this document, " which was kindly lent me by the President of the Society. I compared both " manuscripts carefully at my leisure, and find that the Moncrief manuscript is " by no means a literal copy. There are in the Thompson manuscript over " twelve hundred (1200 !) words additional, omitted, or changed." I underlined in the Thompson manuscript all the passages differing from the Moncrief, and placed it in the hands of the printer, with the request that he would put all the underlined portion into Italics, which he has done. I have counted the words in the "Thompson Journal," and find that as nearly as possible they amount to 11,983. The Moncrief contains somewhat less ; but both contain 10,783 exactly alike. The chief difference arises where whole and sometimes long sentences, which are not found in Moncrief, are found in Thompson ; but all of them, it will be seen, add to the clearness and precision of the narrative. Having my confidence in the integrity and veracity of the Thompsons increased by the enquiries, I cannot hesitate to view the manuscript in my possession as emanating from Mr. James Thompson, junr.; but without reference to the authorship, I now publish it as being the most succinct and clear narrative of the events that occurred during that most momentous crisis of our Canadian history.

WM. JAS. ANDERSON.

QUEBEC, GRANDE ALLÉE,
    21st *October*, 1872.

THE EXPEDITION AGAINST QUEBEC,

IN THE YEAR 1759,

UNDER COMMAND OF MAJOR-GENERAL JAMES WOLFE.

1759.

APRIL.—Louisburg was appointed the place of rendezvous for assembling the Forces destined for the service of this Expedition ; but, as the harbor might not be open early enough, Halifax, which is within a short run of it, was likewise appointed for the same purpose ; and then, the first steps in America relating to that Service were taken.

The first accounts of the intended expedition came to Halifax in the beginning of *the month* of April, and a Squadron of eight men-of-war of the Line, which had wintered there under the command of Admiral Durells, began to prepare for a cruize in the Gulph and River *of* Saint Lawrence.

APRIL 8TH.—The Honorable Brigadier-General Murray, who was appointed to the Staff, being *at* Halifax, in Garrison, made an application to Brigadier-General Lawrence, the Governor, for providing such necessaries for the Service of the *Siege* as might be procured there to advantage, and conveniently transported. The Governor readily complied with *his* demand, and, without loss of time, gave directions accordingly.

APRIL 22ND.—The Honorable Brigadier-General Monkton, the second in Command, arrived from the Continent, *who,* being made acquainted with the particulars to be provided, approved of their being forwarded.

APRIL 30TH.—Admiral Saunders arrived with a fleet from England : he had made attempts to *get* into Louisburg, but was prevented by the Ice, which still remained in great quantities along that coast. Major-General Wolfe, Commander-in-Chief of the Expedition ; the Honble. Brigadier-General Townshend ; and Colonel Carleton, Depy.-Quar.-Masr.-Genl., with some other officers, arrived in the fleet.

This evening there was a detachment of 650 men from the garrison of Halifax, 2 Engineers, a proportion of intrenching Tools, an officer and a small detachment of Artillery, with a couple of Field-pieces, under the command of Col. Carleton, ordered on board *of* Admiral Durell's Fleet, which still remained in the harbor, and now in readiness to sail. This command was to take post *on* one of the islands of the *river* which should be most advantageous for preventing succors from *getting* to the Enemy.

MAY 2ND.—The preparations begun at Halifax were approved of by the General, and, with some other additional articles, ordered to be forwarded with all *possible* dispatch ; and the fleet from England began to refit and water with diligence.

MAY 3RD.—Admiral Durell's Fleet sailed this morning down the harbor ; but, the wind proving contrary, they were obliged to anchor at Maigri's Beach, where they remained till the 5th, and then got to Sea.

MAY 13TH.—This morning Admiral Saunders sailed for Louisburg with all the ships that were in readiness. We met Admiral Holmes off Cape Sambro' with two Ships, the " Somerset" and " Terrible." These ships having met with rough weather at sea, and sustained some damage, were ordered into Halifax to refit. Admiral Holmes hoisted his Flag *on* board the . . . . and proceeded with us to

Louisbourg. Brigr.-Genl. Monkton remained at Halifax to
see that Garrison embark, and to forward some particulars
relating to the Expedition.

MAY 15TH.—In the morning we made Cape Canseau ;
about noon we made the island of Cape Breton, the coast
of which was still full of ice; in the evening we got into
Louisbourg Harbor, where we found the " Bedford" and
" Prince Frederick," *that* had wintered there, and the
" Northumberland," lately arrived from England.

MAY 17TH.—The " Nightingale" and convoy, with Fraser's
Highlanders, arrived from New York. The General ordered
such further necessaries as were not already provided at this
place, with all possible dispatch.

The Troops were now coming in daily, as the weather
permitted, which was often so foggy that many vessels must
have run ashore upon the Coast if the noise of the surf had
not apprised them of their danger. The easterly winds which
brought the fogs brought likewise great quantities of ice, and
made the navigation still more *dangerous*. The harbor of
Louisbourg was so full for several days, that there was no
getting on board *nor* ashore without a great deal of trouble
and danger.

MAY 31ST.—Brigr.-Genl. Monkton arrived with four
Battalions from Halifax and two Battalions from the Bay of
Fundy. Our whole force was now assembled, consisting of
ten Battalions, three Companies of Grenadiers from the
garrison *of* Louisbourg, a detachment of Artillery, and five
companies of Rangers,—the whole amounting to Eight
thousand five hundred and thirty-five men fit for Duty,
officers included (8,535) : they were proportioned on board
of the Transports to the best advantage, and were landed for
air and Exercise, when the weather permitted, during our
stay ; and these opportunities were taken to stow the water
and Provisions on board. The transports were divided into

three Divisions, under the command of Brigr.-Generals Monkton, Townshend, and Murray, each on board of a Frigate, with a distinguishing Pendant to lead and repeat the Signals *required*.

JUNE 4TH.—This morning Admiral Saunders sailed out of Louisbourg harbor with as many of the fleet as could follow ; but the wind coming contrary soon afterwards, *there was a considerable part* left behind, and remained *until the 6th in the morning*, during which time the Admiral kept in the offing ; then the remaining part came out, and the whole *sailed* in the evening.

JUNE 9TH.—Being off the " Bird-Island," we were joined by another company of Rangers, of about 100 men, from the Bay of Fundy.

JUNE 18TH.—In the evening we came to *an* Anchor, for the first time since we left Louisbourg, at the Isle of " Bic." From this island we were for the most part obliged to take *the* advantage of the *tides of flood* and daylight, as the currents began to be strong and the channel narrow. About this time we had accounts by a small vessel taken by one of Admiral Durell's cruizers that a French Fleet got up the river before admiral Durell's arrival, consisting of three Frigates and about twenty sail of Transports, with Recruits, Clothing, Ammunition, Provisions and Merchandize.

JUNE 26TH.—In the evening the last Division of our Transports passed through the " Traverse" at the lower end of the " Isle d'Orléans," which, though reckoned dangerous, our ships *worked* up with a contrary wind. This piece of seamanship surprised the Enemy a good deal, for we were perhaps the first that ever attempted to get through in that manner ; indeed, there were boats with flags anchored upon the *shores* on each side of the channel, which was a necessary precaution with *so* unfavorable winds. It must be observed that we found the navigation of the Saint Lawrence much less difficult than we could have expected from the accounts given of it. Out of our great fleet, consisting of *nearly* two hundred sail, there was not a single ship lost, nor any damage sustained, except the loss of a few anchors and cables where there were strong currents and foul ground. The weather had been pretty moderate ever since our departure, which, no doubt, contributed to this part of our good fortune.

In our way up, we found one of Admiral Durell's squadron at anchor near " Green Island;" the admiral himself, with some *others*, in the North channel of the " Isle-aux-Coudres," and two or three in the South channel of the "Isle d'Orléans." *The three-deck'd ships were left in the North channel of the Isle-aux-Coudres, in case there might not be water enough* for their getting through the " Traverse."

June 27th.—In the morning the signal was made in the South channel of the Isle d'Orléans, off the Church of "Saint Laurent," for landing the Troops: this was immediately set about, and met with no opposition, the island having been abandoned some time before. While the Troops were disembarking, the General went *with an Escort to the point of Orléans*, called by the French "Bout-de-l'isle, and saw the Enemy encamped along the North shore of the Bason, in eight different encampments, extending from the " *Rivière* Saint Charles" to within one mile of the "*Sault* Montmorenci," and the coast fortified all along as far as the encampments reached. There were some floating batteries, launches, and batteaux, with cannon, in the creeks along the shore. These precautions in the Enemy were plain indications that the most advantageous landing, and the most practicable, must be upon that coast. There was no judging, with certainty, of the Enemy's strength from the extent and number of their encampments; but we had good intelligence that they were about 15,000 or 16,000 men!

B

After taking a full view of all that could be seen from this place, the General returned to "Saint Laurent," and ordered the Troops then disembarked to Encamp. The 3rd Batallion of Royal Americans remained on board till further orders.

In the afternoon there came on a heavy gale of wind at North-East, which occasioned a good deal of damage amongst our Transports, and, as we afterwards learned, gave the enemy very favorable hopes of an easy riddance. If it had come on in the night-time, or continued some hours longer, it might, in some measure, have answered their expectations. We, however, escaped without losing any ship. Some few vessels had run ashore, but were afterwards got off; and the only loss we felt sensibly was that of our Boats, which affected our motions throughout the whole campaign.

JUNE 28TH.—About eleven at night the enemy sent 7 Fire-ships from the Town to go down the S. Channel *with the ebb-tide* and burn our fleet; but they managed so as to entertain us instead of annoying us. They set them on fire, and left them to the direction of the current before they *had* got within half a mile of our head-most ship, which gave our boats time to grapple and tow them ashore, tho' all in flames; and there they burnt down without touching a single ship.

JUNE 29TH.—In the morning Colonel Carleton was sent, with *three Companies of Grenadiers* from St. Laurent, to encamp on the Point of Orléans. In the evening Brigr.-Genl. Monkton crossed the South channel from Saint Laurent to "Beaumont," with four Battalions, three companies of Light Infantry, and some Rangers, and marched from thence next morning, and in the evening took possession of "Pointe-Levi." In that march his advanced and flank-parties exchanged some few shots with some of the Enemy's scouting-parties, and picked up a box of papers belonging to their Commanding-

Officer, which led to some discoveries. Pointe-Levi was immediately *began* to be fortified, and was kept for an hospital and a place of arms during the Campaign.

JULY 2ND.—There were three Battalions sent from Saint Laurent to encamp at the Point of Orléans, under the Command of Brigr.-General Townshend. This place was likewise *began to be fortified* for a place of arms and an Hospital, and kept so during the Campaign. Here the General, for the present, fixed his Head-Quarters.

JULY 3RD.—The remainder of the Army of St. Laurent came to the Point of Orléans, under the Command of Brigr.-Genl. Murray.

JULY 4TH.—Brigr.-Genl. Murray went up the South side of the river, towards the " *Etchemins,*" to reconnoitre and take a view of the opposite side, *above the Town :* upon his return there was a place fixed for landing there, and some rafts for ferrying the Troops across the river were ordered to be made at Pointe-Levi ; but that plan was soon after laid aside.

JULY 5TH.—The 48th Battalion, with three companies of Light Infantry and some Rangers, under the command of Colonel Burton, were encamped and *cantoned* near " Pointe des Pères," to cover some works and batteries ordered this day by the General to be erected there, against the Town.

JULY 8TH.—The General, with the Grenadiers of the army, six companies of Light Infantry, and two of Rangers, marched from the Camp at the Point of Orléans at eight in the evening, and between eleven and twelve *at night* crossed the *North* channel, a little above *the Church of* " *Saint Pierre,*" and about two *o'clock* next morning took possession of the ground upon the East side of the Falls of " Montmorency." He was followed the same night by the three Battals. under the command of Brigr.-Genl. Townshend.

There was no opposition made to our taking possession of *this* ground ; and it seems probable that the Enemy did not discover us until day-light next morning, for, by the stir then in their camp, they seemed to be somewhat alarmed. This camp was immediately *began* to be fortified, and here the General fixed his Head-Quarters while he *kept* possession of it.

July 11th.—In the morning we discovered that the Enemy had, in the night-*time*, began to advance their breast-works upon the edge of the bank, towards the falls. This night Brigr.-General Murray brought the remainder of our Army, which still lay at the Point of Orléans, to the Camp at Montmorenci, having left that Post to be guarded by a detachment of Marines landed for the purpose.

July 12th.—There were two Batteries opened against the Town at " Pointe *des* Pères"—one of six 32-pounders, the other of five 13-in. mortars.

July 16th.—A carcass from our Battery set the Town on fire on the North side of the Jesuits' *College, in the street "La Fabrique," and* burned for several hours.

July 19th.—This night the Sutherland · and some Transports passed the Town with the 3rd Battalion of Royal Americans, with some other Troops on board under the Command of Colonel Carleton, *which* we understood *by* deserters had alarmed the Enemy a good deal.

July 20th.—There was another Battery opened against the Town at Pointe *des* Pères of 4 Sea-Service Mortars—three of 13 inches and one of 10 inches,—it having been found by a trial made that a Bomb-Ketch could not lay her broadside to the Town for the strength of the current ; the sea-mortars were, therefore, employed by land.

July 21st.—There was a descent made at " Pointe-aux-Trembles," seven leagues above the Town, on the North side, by Colonel Carleton. His party was fired upon at first landing by some Canadians and Indians, but they were soon dispersed. He took possession of some Plans and Papers, a good many Women, and a few men Prisoners. Major Prevost, with 1 or 2 more officers and a few private *men*, were wounded, and a few other privates killed.

JULY 22ND.—At night there was a considerable fire in the Town, caused by a Carcass, which burnt the Cathedral and ten or twelve good houses in its neighbourhood.

JULY 26TH.—About three o'clock this morning, the General and Brig.-General Murray, with the 35th Regiment, five Companies of Light-Infantry and one of the Rangers, and two field-pieces, set out from Montmorenci-Camp to reconnoitre two fords about five miles *above* the Falls. After we had proceeded about a mile and a-half, the field-pieces were sent back to Camp, the *ground* being too bad to get them on. About half-way between the camp and the ford the road passes through a remarkable ravine, which is about 300 yards long, very narrow, and the banks on each side above 20 feet high, and so steep as to admit of no outlet but where the road *passes*. Upon the march we were frequently challenged by the Enemy from the opposite side of the river, for they observed all our movements with great vigilance. Upon our coming to the nearest ford we found they had a breast-work of considerable extent upon the opposite Bank. On our side of the river there was an open space of ground with a house in the centre of it; and on the left of this opening the road to the ford passes through woods. Our Troops were now drawn up, to be in readiness in case of being attacked, the 35th across the road, and the Light-Infantry upon the right along the Skirts of........opening, the whole so far in the woods as to be concealed. The ford and the Enemy's works and Position were then reconnoitred, and the company of Rangers with a French deserter was sent to reconnoitre the other Ford, which is about a mile higher up. Between 8 and 9 o'clock there were about thirty

Canadians and Indians seen going into the House, upon which there was a platoon of the 35th ordered through the woods between them and the river, to attack them. Just as the platoon marched off it was fired upon, and the officer wounded by those very people, who had by this time got roun(' them into the woods. But the platoon being joined oy a Company of Light-Infantry, they were soon beaten back across the River. There was *then* an Ambuscade laid, in case of a second attack, which was by posting a Company of Light-Infantry on an advanced eminence near the river, in the woods, and below the opening, with orders, if attacked, to retreat back along the road, which would lead the enemy, if they pursued, into the fire of the Battalion, and give a fair chance of cutting off their retreat with the Light-Infantry. There were two other advantageous Eminences taken possession of at the same time,—one with two Companies on our left flank, near the River, and the other with one Company in the rear of the same flank, upon the right of the Road. About one o'clock a detachment of fifteen hundred Canadians and Indians crossed the river a considerable way *above* the opening, and, marching down unperceived, under cover of its banks, got up a ravine upon the right of the advanced Light-Infantry *company mentioned.* The officer commanding that company kept them in play till he called in his sentries, and then retreated, according to Orders; but the Enemy, instead of pursuing him, as was expected, along the road, endeavored to gain the height where the three companies were posted. When they got near it, the two Companies, *unperceived,* wheeled and attacked their flank, which being quite unexpected, they instantly turned their backs; and the Light-Infantry coming upon their rear at the same time, they were soon driven into the river, *where they* suffered very considerably in crossing, being quite open to our fire. We did not learn the number of their killed and wounded ; but the Indians were dispirited, from *this* day's loss, for all the rest of the Campaign.

We had fifty-five men killed and wounded, officers included.,
Our chief loss was in pursuing the Enemy home to the river
from the Breastworks upon the opposite *banks*, where their
numbers, exclusive of those that attacked *us*, amounted, as
we were afterwards informed, to two thousand five hundred
men! After burying the dead, our detachment was ordered
to carry off the wounded and return to Camp, which was
effected without molestation. This Ford is about 150 yards
broad and about 4 feet deep; the water is smooth, *and not
rapid.* The opposite bank is very steep and the path-way
narrow. The other ford reconnoitred by the Rangers is
between 2 and three hundred yards broad ; in passing it there
are some islands to cross in the middle of the river. The
bottom is smooth and the water shallow, with a gentle
current. The road to it on the Coast-side passes through a
morass covered with thick wood, and almost impracticable,
which is probably the reason why the Enemy gave so litt'e
attention to it, for they had neither men nor works there.
From these fords there is another road which leads to
" L'Ange Gardien." This day two of the Enemy's Floating
Batteries were taken in the mouth of the " Chaudière" River,
by our boats above the Town. The hands belonging to them
got ashore and escaped, after having wounded some few
of our men in the attack. We had always found this *sort*
of craft very troublesome, so that these two were no
unwelcome prize, tho' otherwise of little value.

JULY 28TH.—About one o'clock in the morning there was
a long chain of Fire-rafts (*Cajeux*) launched from " Beauport"
to go down the South Channel and make a second trial
of burning our Fleet; but it ended as the former, all in show.
Without doing any damage, they were towed ashore on the
island of Orleans. This day there was another Battery
opened against the Town at Pointe des Pères, of six
24-pounders.

JULY 31ST.—There was a descent made upon the coast
of Beauport, about three-quarters of a mile above the mouth

of the Montmorenci, the particulars of which are as follows: About ten in the morning, it being then high-water, there were two vessels run aground where the descent was intended, mounting 14 guns each. They had on board 3 Companies of Grenadiers, 2 Engineers, a detachment of Artillery, 2 Field-pieces, 1000 Intrenching Tools, with some Fascines and Pickets. They were to have been placed so as to have made their Fire bear upon the Easternmost of the two Redoubts next the Falls, which was to have been the first attacked.

The "Centurion," *a 60-gun ship*, went soon afterwards down the North Channel, and was to have been placed so as to *have her* fire bear on the Easternmost of these two Redoubts, to prevent its annoying two Brigades that were to ford across the mouth of the Montmorenci, at Low-water, to join the attack; but all the three were placed to some disadvantage. The Westernmost vessel was too far from *the* object; and the Easternmost, altho' near enough, lay too obliquely, heeled from her fire when the tide fell, and was raked fore-and-aft by the Easternmost redoubt; *and* the "Centurion" had dropt down at least 500 yards too far. They, however, fired as fast as their guns would allow, and were joined by our Artillery from Montmorenci camp.

The Landing was to have been in the following order:—The Grenadiers on board the vessels, commanded by Lieut.-Colo. Murray, *from the point of Orléans, and four pickets of the 2nd Battn.* Royal Americans, from Montmorenci, commanded by Colonel Burton, were to make the First Attack. They were to be joined by Amherst's and Fraser's, from Pointe Lévi, commanded by Brigadr.-General Monkton; and the two brigades from Montmorenci, commanded by Brigadr.-Generals Townshend and Murray, were to sustain the whole.

The Picketts from Montmorenci and the Troops from Orléans and Pointe Lévi were in their boats about eleven o'clock, the tide then beginning to fall; when they had got about mid-channel, there came orders *to keep laying* upon their Oars, *it being too* early in the Tide for the Brigades from Montmorenci to cross the Ford. The Enemy's Batteries playing now very warmly upon the *two* armed vessels, it was considered that the Grenadiers on board suffered to no purpose ; there were boats, *therefore,* sent to take them off, with orders to join the rest. Between 3 and 4 in the afternoon there came orders for going on, in the execution of which some of the boats with the Grenadiers ran aground ; but the men could not land, there being too great a depth of water between them and the shore ; and as they had got within reach of the Enemy's cannon, the whole were called off, but kept *playing as* before. The Enemy were now sufficiently apprised of our design, and had time enough to be prepared accordingly. Their intrenchments on the edge of the Bank were fully manned for a considerable way, and the greatest part of the remainder of their Troops under arms, between the Church of Beauport and the place of attack, ready to move as occasion should require. They had kept firing all day upon our Boats with both Cannon and Mortars, but with very little execution.

About a quarter past five there came second orders for going on, which were soon executed, tho' the boats were much dispersed, particularly as they expected no further service that day. The Grenadiers and Picketts landed very quickly, formed as fast as they could, but pushed forward *rather* too eagerly to the attack of the Westernmost Redoubt and Battery. They had proceeded but a very little way when the Enemy began a close heavy fire with small arms from their intrenchments on the top of the Bank, which had an entire command of the ground where the redoubt stood : they, however, got possession of it, *the enemy having abandoned it ;* but they were so much exposed to the enemy's fire, which continued very steady, that they were obliged to retreat. This they did without firing a shot; but their order was otherwise somewhat broken. Then they began to form in the rear of the two Battalions from Pointe Levi, which had

c

landed immediately after them, and were then drawn up under cover of the two armed vessels. The two Brigades from Montmorenci had by this time got within half a mile of us, to a place appointed, where General Townshend halted and sent for orders.

Everything was now ready for a second attack ; *but it was thought too late : the* tide was coming in, *and but little daylight remaining ; the former of which circumstances must,* in about an hour, cut off all possibility of a retreat by the ford, *and the latter prevent* our reaping any considerable advantage from a victory, if we obtained one. It was, therefore, ordered that the two Brigades from Montmorenci should recross the Ford. Amherst's re-embarked for Pointe Levi ; the Grenadiers and Picketts for the Point of Orléans ; and Fraser's to bring up the rear to Montmorency Camp, where the General himself went. These movements were made with great order, altho' within reach of the Enemy's Cannon, which must have done a good deal of execution had they been well served.

There was a party of Fraser's left on board the Easternmost vessel until the tide *got round both* her and the other. The party, with the wounded and sailors on board, were then withdrawn, and both the vessels set on fire, that there might be as little as possible left *that could be of use to* the Enemy.

Our loss was between forty and fifty killed, and between three and four hundred wounded. Of the latter were Colonel Burton and Lieut.-Colo. Murray.

The Enemy were said to have lost about sixty men by our cannon. We fired no small arms *until the order for our retreat,* which had, as we afterwards learned, given the Enemy no small opinion of the *discipline of our Troops.* About this time there was a Manifesto published by the General, setting forth that such Canadians as should continue in Arms after the tenth of August should have their habitations burnt, and all hostilities allowable by the rules of War put in execution against them.

AUGUST 5TH.—Brigadier-General Murray went up the south side of the River with the 15th Regiment, four companies of Light-Infantry, and two hundred marines. He embarked on board our fleet, commanded by Admiral Holmes. His whole Command (including the 3rd Battn. Royal Americans, which had been on board before,) consisted of about twelve hundred men. He was to destroy a magazine at " Deschambault," and assist our Fleet to attack that of the Enemy at " Richelieu."

AUGUST 9TH.—About one o'clock this morning, our carcasses *at* Pointe Levi set the lower Town on fire in two different places; by eight o'clock it was burnt to ashes, all but four or five houses. We found afterwards, by some accounts in intercepted letters, that this and the former fire mentioned had *burnt* one hundred and eighty houses of the best in the Town !

AUGUST 13TH.—The General gave Orders for augmenting the Battery at Point-*des*-Pères to forty pieces of cannon. This was thought to *have been concluded upon either to favor a storming by* water *or to do the Town all possible damage if it could not be taken, which now became doubtful, as there was little or no appearance of making good a landing* upon a coast naturally strong, and *so thoroughly* fortified, and defended by *such* superior numbers.

AUGUST 17TH.—A volunteer, posted with a Sergeant, Corporal, and sixteen men, in a house below the *Falls* of Montmorenci-Camp, *stood* an attack by upwards of one hundred Canadians and Indians for nearly two hours. *Succors* then *arriving* from Camp, *the enemy betook themselves to* flight, and narrowly escaped *being surrounded;* several *of them* were killed, but none taken. The volunteer was, by Public Orders, appointed to the first vacant Commission for his gallant behavior.

August 23rd.—We began to burn the habitations between "Saint Joachim" and the Falls of Montmorenci, agreeably to the Manifesto lately published.

August 25th.—Brigr.-General Murray returned to the camp at Pointe-Lévi with his Command, mention'd the 5th *instant.* He brought the first accounts of Niagara, *Carillon,* and Crown-Point being taken. His transactions up the river were as follows :—The 8th, he made two attempts to land at Pointe-aux-Trembles, to favor the seamen in cutting-off three floating-*batteries* which lay on the North shore. The first was made at low-water, which, he was informed, was the most *proper* time, as he could have room to form on the beach, out of the reach of the Enemy's Fire ; but a landing at low-water proved impracticable, there *being* ledges of rock along the shore which boats *cannot* pass, *and* with gulleys and ponds of water between them and the shore, which the men could not *pass* without wetting their ammunition. When this attempt was made, the Enemy *shewed* about five hundred men. The second attempt was made at high-water. The Enemy kept pretty much concealed until we got almost ashore, and then opened *with* such a heavy fire of small-arms that the sailors could not sit to their oars. *There was a* diversion made to the right, to divide their fire, which in some measure answered ; but it still continued too hot to face it during a Landing. The numbers of the Enemy were greatly increased : the woods were everywhere lined ; all the houses of the village occupied ; a considerable body of Regulars drawn up behind the Church, and a Body of Cavalry dismounted near the shore. These circumstances made it more than probable that the attempt, if pursued further, would be attended with considerable loss, without any prospect of success : it was, therefore, ordered to retreat. We had about one hundred and forty men killed and wounded, including thirty seamen. The Troops were immediately re-embarked on board the respective ships ! The 9th, at night, an officer with a small party surprised a *party* of twenty-five Canadians on the south shore. He took five prisoners, and killed and wounded *several* more, without any loss on our side. The 10th, in the morning, the whole detachment landed on the South shore, in the parish of Saint Antoine ; the landing was opposed by about one hundred and fifty Canadians and fifty Indians, who were soon *drawn off*. There *were several of them killed and wounded*. The whole detachment encamped here upon a spot of ground above the Church. The 12th, there was a detachment of four hundred men, under the command of major Dalling, ordered to proceed at *one* o'clock next morning and surprise the back concession of Saint Antoine. They were fired upon before day-break, and had a captain and four men wounded by some of the inhabitants, who went off immediately after; upon which there was a *paper posted* up on the Church-door to *acquaint them* that since they had fired several times upon our Troops, notwithstanding General Wolfe's Manifesto, all the houses in the Parish should be burnt ; that the Church only should be saved, but should undergo the same fate if they continued *making signals* from it. The houses were accordingly burnt *that day and the day following.* The 17th, at about eight at night, the land-troops re-embarked ; the marines remained in camp in a strong redoubt, with orders to make the usual number of fires that night, and all the show they could the next *day.* About eleven, the Troops proceeded in the flat-bottomed Boats for Deschambault, which is eight leagues higher up on the North shore. About an hour after day-break, next morning, they landed, without opposition, at " Portneuf," which is a league below; then marched and took possession of the Magazine ; and, having posted a party there, with Orders to touch nothing on pain of Death, marched forward and took possession of the Church, *which is a little higher up. Upon a movement of the Light-Infantry to surround a small party of the enemy that seemed disposed to dispute the way to the Church, they went off without firing a shot.* The magazine was now examined, and, being found to contain nothing but military stores and Baggage, was set on fire. Whilst it continued burning, there were about *fifty* different explosions of gunpowder, by which two neighboring houses, *not intended to be burnt, were set on fire.* We then re-embarked (about six in the evening) without the loss of a man, although fired at all day. The superiority of our fire-arms *kept* the enemy at too great a distance to do us any injury. After embarking, there were two boats of Amherst's and the two floating-batteries (taken from the enemy some time ago) sent to burn a Brigantine. The enemy ran her aground and abandoned her. Our boats set her on fire soon afterwards, and attended until the tide left her *dry,* and she burnt down. The enemy's ships made no attempt to save her, although it was thought they might have done so without running any risk, for they lay only about three miles above her. The attack upon the Enemy's shipping, which was one of the designs of the Expedition, was laid aside, our sea-officers *having* found difficulties to exist that must have prevented our ships from getting so high up. General Murray, therefore, with his Command, returned, as already mentioned, but left the 3rd Battalion of Royal Americans on board the fleet, where he found them.

August 28th.—About one, this morning, the Lowestoff Frigate and some more vessels passed above the Town. There was a battery of eight 12-pounders opened this day at Pointe-*des*-Pères.

August 31st.—This night, the Seahorse Frigate and *four* Transports passed above the Town.

September 3rd.—The General *broke' up Camp from* Montmorenci this day about noon. The Redoubts, Batteries, and other works *were set on* fire last night and this morning. It was expected that the Enemy, *who* for some days past must have observed our preparations for leaving *Camp,* would have attacked our Retreat ; but they made no attempt that way. The General *wanted* they should, and laid a *temptation* for that purpose, but which did not take. He ordered the several corps to their *respective* alarm-posts *in* the night, and to conceal themselves after day-light, excepting a few guards *that* were to appear very alert; but *Monsieur de Montcalm*, the French General, contrary to the opinion of his officers, saw something about our camp which gave him a suspicion of the affair, and made him decline *an attempt.* A few hours discovered that his suspicion was *well-founded ;* but it was a pretty general opinion that he might have made the attempt—to great advantage, at all events.

The fortifying of this Camp, and bringing so many pieces of Artillery to it, was a work of great Labor *to our men.* There were about fifty pieces there *at one time ;* and altho' there was no loss of men in taking *possession of* or leaving the place, yet during our stay we suffered a good deal. Our Fascine and covering-parties were frequently attacked; and altho' we always repulsed the Enemy, yet it was seldom without some little loss, which in the *aggregate* amounted to a considerable number. These skirmishes had, indeed, the effect of using our men to the woods, and familiarising them with the *mode of warfare peculiar to* the Canadians and Indians, whom they began to despise.

The General ordered the Troops from this Camp to encamp along the road in rear of the batteries at Pointe-des-Pères, excepting the 2nd Battalion of Royal Americans, which was left at the Point of Orléans. He now fixed his Head-Quarters at Pointe-Lévi.

SEPTEMBER 4TH.—Dispatches from General Amherst, by an officer and four rangers, brought a confirmation of the taking of Niagara, Carillon, and Crown Point.

SEPTEMBER 5TH.—This evening, Brigr.-General Murray went up the South side of the River from Pointe-Lévi camp with four Battalions, and embarked between the Etchemins and Chaudière rivers on board our Fleet, then lying off that place. This fleet consisted of the " Sutherland," of 60 guns, the " Lowestoff," " Seahorse" and " Squirrel" Frigates and " Hunter" Sloop, with two or three small armed vessels and some Transports ; the whole under the Command of Admiral Holmes.

This afternoon, Brigr.-Generals Monkton and Townshend, with three Battalions, marched from Pointe-Lévi, and embarked in the same place that General Murray did the night before. The General followed in the evening, and embarked likewise. He left the 2nd Battalion of Royal Americans and some Marines, under the Command of Colonel Carleton, to keep possession of the Post at the Point of Orléans. He left the 48th Regiment, some small detachments of. other corps, and some Marines, under the command of Colonel Burton, to keep the batteries at Pointe-*des*-Pères and the Camp at Pointe-Lévi.

SEPTEMBER 7TH.—Early this morning the Fleet moved up to " Caprouge," and in the evening, the General, having reconnoitred the Coast, fixed upon a place, a little below Pointe-aux-Trembles, for making a descent; but the weather not proving favorable at the time ordered, which was *the 9th, in the morning,* it was put off, and the Troops, being so much crowded on board the Transports, were that evening landed at " Saint-Nicolas," on the south side, for air and exercise. The General, upon the same day, *discovered* another place more to his mind *for the purposes of a Descent,* and laid aside all further thoughts of that at Pointe-aux-Trembles.

SEPT. 10TH.—The General took with him Admiral Holmes and Brigadiers-General Monkton and Townshend, with some other officers, to reconnoitre the place he had fixed upon ; Brigadier-General Murray *being* left ashore with the command of the Troops at Saint-Nicolas. The place fixed upon is called "Foulon." They reconnoitred it from a rising ground on the South side of the River, below the mouth of the Etchemin river, from whence they *had* 'a fair view, not only of the place itself, but likewise of a considerable part of the ground between it and the Town, which is a mile and a-half below. *As the place is laid down upon the Plan, it requires little or no description ; but it must be observed* that the Bank which runs along the Shore is very steep and woody, and was thought so impracticable by the French themselves, that they had then only a single Pickett to defend it. This Pickett (where we supposed there were about one hundred men) was encamped upon the Bank, near the top of a narrow winding path which runs up from the shore. This path was broken up by the Enemy themselves, and barricaded with an abbatis; but about two hundred yards to the right, there appeared to be a slope in the bank which it was thought might answer the purpose.

These circumstances, *joined* to the distance of the place from succors, seemed to promise a fair chance of success.

SEPTEMBER 11TH.—There were Orders for the Troops ashore to embark the *next morning*, and for the whole to hold themselves in readiness to land on the 13th, before day-break. The first landing was to consist of four hundred Light Infantry, under the Command of Colonel Howe, and thirteen hundred of the Regiments Bragg, Kenedy, Anstruther, Lascelles, and a detachment of Fraser's, under *the command* of Generals Monkton and Murray, both Commands amounting to *seventeen hundred* men, which was the *whole* number our boats *were enabled to land* at one trip. The *vessels* that had the Troops *for* the second landing, on board, were to follow the boats and *come to* an anchor as near the landing-place as possible. These consisted of three Frigates, a man-of-war sloop, three armed vessels, and two Transports. They were to be followed by some Ordnance-vessels with Intrenching-tools, Artillery and Ammunition.

D

The second landing was to consist of Amherst's Louisbourg *volunteers* (Grenadiers), the remainder of Fraser's, a detachment of Light Infantry, the 3rd Battalion of Royal Americans, and Otway's, the whole amounting to nineteen hundred and ten men, under the Command of Brigr.-Genl. Townshend.

September 12th.—The Troops that had been ashore re-embarked in *consequence* of yesterday's orders, and every *preparation made to put in train* the business of the day following. There were injunctions given both *to* officers and men *in every way* suitable to the *approaching* occasion. The *sea*-officers who were to conduct the boats in the landing were likewise thoroughly instructed in their part of that duty. Our Fleet still continued at anchor off Caprouge, which is about six miles above Foulon. The "Hunter" sloop lay about two-thirds of the way further down. The Enemy had a body of between two and three thousand men, including two hundred and thirty Horse, under the Command of Monsieur Bougainville, a brevet-Colonel, posted from Caprouge-river along the Coast towards Pointe-aux-Trembles, to watch our motions and to prevent our making a descent at these places, which they *suspected* to have been our design. They had some batteaux in the mouth of that river with cannon, and a sloop run a little way up, so that they wanted no advantage *towards* making an immediate discovery of every step we could take, whether by night or day.

September 13th.—Between two and three in the morning our boats began to be in motion, dropping down with the tide in the order *in which they were to land*, mentioned before, and as silently as they could. Admiral Holmes hoisted his Flag on board of one of the Frigates, and followed with the shipping in the same manner; the whole seemingly unobserved by the Enemy. In our way down, a captain of the Light-Infantry in one of *our head-most* boats discovered by accident from the Hunter sloop that the enemy expected

some boats that night down the river with Provisions, and,
availing himself of the discovery (*and his knowledge of the
French language*), passed several of the enemy's sentries as
such, by which *means* the Light-Infantry had actually landed
without being once fired at. The Battalions under Brigadier-
Generals Monkton and Murray landed immediately after
them, and then the Enemy's Pickett took the alarm and
began to fire.

Three companies of Light-Infantry were immediately
ordered to get up the bank, to the right of the pathway, as
they could, and to give a signal when *they got up*, upon
which the remainder of the Light-Infantry were to force the
pathway and attack the Pickett in front; but after a little
firing that Pickett was *dislodged and dispersed* by the three
Companies only. The French Captain was wounded and
(with about half his pickett) *taken* prisoner ; the remainder
made their escape along the edge of the bank, towards the
Town, and, with some flying-parties posted there, kept firing
upon some of our boats that had by mistake dropped down
too far that way, *when the General followed* in his own boat to
order them back.

The Battalions were .formed upon the Beach as they
landed, and now began to *climb* up the bank and form *on
the summit.* The Light-Infantry *was* disposed of, some in the
woods on our left flank, to cover that side, and others to
scour the face of the Bank towards the Town.

The General, being now landed, gave orders to *expedite* the
getting-up of some troops still remaining below ; and a guard
being left to cover the remainder of the Landing, he *gained*
the summit of the bank about day-break. Very soon after his
getting up, a pickett of the Battn. of " Guianne" appeared
upon a rising ground at some little distance above us ; but,
finding they were too late, they retired without making any
attempt to molest us. By information we afterwards

obtained, *it appeared the whole Battalion of Guianne was to have been posted on this* ground the night before ; *but by intelligence received from a deserter by the French General,* that there was a descent to be made by us that night on the coast of Beauport, *he (fortunately for us) deferred the measure.*

All the Troops of the first landing being now got upon the top of the bank, the first step taken was the attack of a battery of four pieces of Cannon which the enemy had at a place called " Samosse," about a mile and a-half above, and near " Sillerie." This Battery began to play about day-break, and must have annoyed both boats and shipping a good deal, particularly those of *Brigadier-General Murray, with the* 58th *Regiment.* The Light-Infantry, under the Command of Colonel Howe, was immediately sent to surround it, with two *French* Deserters as guides. *Brigr.-General Murray followed to the skirts of the woods, where he took post across the road leading to the Battery.*

The main body of the first landing was now marched up to the top of the height called the " Hauteur d'Abraham," which forms a Plain. They found some of the Enemy in a house, and some Indians skulking in a coppice hard-by. *There was* a detachment of Grenadiers sent to beat them off, which, after exchanging a few shot, they effected ; then the whole were drawn up with the right to the Town and *facing* "Saint Louis" Road. They remained but a short time in this position, when the General, from an eminence on the right, discovered the Enemy assembling upon the rising grounds between him and the Town ; and, observing their numbers *to be fast increasing, he altered the position of his Line,* and faced towards them. He sent for *Brigadier-*General Murray to return and join him with the 58th Regiment, and for Colonel Howe, with the Light-Infantry, to come and cover his rear. The Order soon reached General Murray, who immediately *took up the position assigned to him ;*

but the Light-Infantry having already gone forward, the officer who was the bearer of the order *proceeded (with a platoon of Grenadiers)* as far as the Battery, *and, discovering that Colonel Howe had anticipated the movement, he, by a* short-cut through the woods, *got back to the rear of the army before the Colonel.* The Enemy *at the Battery at Samosse* fired a gun at *the Grenadiers* with a volley of small arms, which was returned ; and the Light-Infantry coming up just at the time, the Enemy abandoned their Battery without making any further resistance. *The General, finding that Colonel Howe had mastered the Battery, sent back a detachment of Twenty Light-Infantry* to keep possession of it.

Both Armies now became pretty numerous—ours by our second landing, which by this time had joined *the first ;* and *theirs by* their Troops from Beauport, and which were *still* coming on very fast. In the *interval* between the two Armies there were clumps of high Bush, *the cover afforded by which brought on a skirmishing, which was* warmly kept up on both sides *while the Troops* were assembling, and the different dispositions making for a general Action. When the lines were nearly completed there began a slight cannonading with small Field-pieces, the Enemy with one in their Line, and we with two in ours. The 48th Regiment and 2nd Battalion of Royal Americans that had marched up from Pointe Levi to the opposite *point*, and crossed over to Foulon, were the last that joined us. They came about eight o'clock, and our line and disposition were completed *very* soon afterwards.

Our Line, consisting of the three Companies of Louisbourg Grenadiers and six Battalions, faced the Enemy's Line,—the Right commanded by Brig.-General Monkton, and the Left by Brigr.-Gen. Murray. The *individual* Corps were Commanded as follows, vizt. :—The Louisbourg Grenadiers by Lieut.-Col. Murray ; the 35th by Lieut.-Col. Fletcher ; the 28th by Colonel Walsh ; the 43rd by Major Elliott ; the 47th by Lieut.-Col. Hale ; the 63rd and 78th by Captain Campbell ; and the 58th by

Major Agnew. The rear of our Left was covered by two Battalions, commanded by Brigr.-General Townshend, which faced the Enemy's Irregulars upon that side. These two Battalions were the 15th, *commanded* by major Irving, and the 2nd Battalion of Royal Americans, *commanded* by Captain Oswald. The 48th, commanded by Colonel Burton (scarcely recovered of his wound), formed a body of Reserve in the rear of the right. Our Light-Infantry, *commanded* by Colonel Howe, covered our rear; and the 3rd Battn. of Royal Americans, commanded by Colonel Young, *covered* the Landing-place, *in order to protect our Boats and secure a means of retreat, which the very great superiority (in numbers) of the Enemy rendered a measure of precaution not to be neglected.* The General moved about *at every point,* but, after the *commencement* of the Action, *kept* on a rising ground *on our right flank,* from whence He had a view of the whole field.

The Enemy's Line was completed soon after ours. It consisted of five Battalions of Regulars in the centre, and of three Battalions of the Colony-Troops on the Right and Left. Their Irregulars, consisting of Canadians and Indians, were dispersed in flying-parties (*voltigeurs*) upon our Flanks, particularly our left, where they were very numerous, and, before the charge *made by* the main body, made some *feeble* advances, as if they *intended* to attack us at *that point;* but General Townshend having ordered two Picketts from the 15th to advance by turn and to fire upon them, *they afterwards kept up only a straggling fire, and at too great a distance to do much execution.*

The Enemy's General Officers were Lieutenant-Général *le Marquis de Montcalm,* and Général de Brigade Sénézergues, Lieutenant-Colonel de Lasarre.

The French Line began moving up to the Charge about nine o'clock, advancing briskly, and for some *short* time in good order; but *before they got within reach, their* front began to Fire, which immediately extended throughout the whole body, in a wild, scattered manner. *They were soon. observed* to waver, *yet continued to advance* with the same disorderly fire.

When they reached to within One hundred yards of us, *our Line moved up slowly* and regularly with a steady pace, and, when within twenty or thirty yards of closing, gave a general *discharge*, upon which the Enemy's whole Line turned *their backs from right to left* in the same instant. They were, by ten o'clock, pursued within musket-shot of their own walls, and scarcely *took a look* behind them until they had got within *the Garrison*.

Their Irregulars upon our left moved towards the Town as soon as their line gave way, but still maintained their ground along the Bank upon that side, where, *being protected* by the Coppice and Brush, they kept up a continued *firing*.

Brigr.-General Murray, who, with Fraser's Battalion of Highlanders (*the 78th*), had pursued the enemy to within musket-shot of Sainte Ursule's Bastion, being informed that all our General-*Officers* were wounded, and the French. having totally *disappeared*, was now returning back to the Field of Battle ; but hearing the firing of Irregulars *to be resumed from the Brushwood*, ordered the *Highlanders to go* and beat them off. A hot skirmishing ensued, in which they (the Highlanders) suffered a good deal ; but, being *at length joined by* a *part* of the 58th Regiment and of the 2nd Battalion of Royal Americáns, they drove *the French down the Bank*, into the suburbs of Saint Rocque, and from thence towards the Bridge on the Saint Charles, where the Main Body, after having passed through the Town to *conceal* their Retreat, were still crossing in great confusion. We then became sole Masters of the Field. Our Loss, although not great in numbers, was nevertheless *very* severe.

Our *General* was *mortally wounded* when the affair had *nearly arrived* to a crisis, and *survived* only long enough *to be made acquainted with the Glorious Tidings, to a true Soldier, " that the cause entrusted to him by His Sovereign and his Country had terminated in* VICTORY."

Brigadier-General Monkton received a very severe wound soon after the *Commanding*-General, and was carried off the field. We had more *casualties from the skirmishing* than in the general action, *in consequence of the proximity of the brushwood, which offered too great an inducement to the Indians to pursue their favorite mode of warfare, the result of which on this occasion proved to be but too favorable.* Of the number wounded was Colonel Carleton (*very severely*), and was carried off the field before the main body of the enemy came to the Charge.

Our Loss upon the whole was nine officers killed and fifty-five wounded ; Forty-nine non-commissioned officers and privates killed and five hundred and forty-two wounded.

The Enemie's loss *exceeded ours in numbers.* The Marquis de Montcalm was mortally wounded ; and Brigr.-General Sénézergues, with about two hundred officers and men, lay dead upon the field. We took thirteen officers and three hundred and *thirty* men Prisoners. The number of their wounded we could not exactly *ascertain ; but from various corroborative accounts they must have exceeded twelve hundred.*

The Command now devolved upon Brigr.-General Townshend, *who was said to be* wounded by mistake in place of Colonel Carleton.

Soon after the *general* action *the enemy* attempted to re-take the Battery at Samosse ; but they were again repulsed, with some loss.

Between twelve and one o'clock there appeared a considerable body of the Enemy upon the Saint-Foix road, in the rear of our left, which we soon learned to be Monsieur

Bougainville's command, *which* we left in the morning at Caprouge. Upon his finding that the main point was already decided, and seeing some of our Battalions in motion, and our Artillery *moving* towards him, he withdrew. The Party that attacked the Battery at Samosse *had been detached from him on the march.*

In the afternoon we began to raise redoubts in the front and upon the flanks of our camp. We lay that night under arms, and sent a detachment to take possession of the " Hôpital-Général ;" and such of the enemy as were wounded that day, and *were found* there, were considered as prisoners of war, the Hospital having *been so near the field of battle.*

SEPTEMBER 14TH AND 15TH.—These two days were taken up in fortifying our Camp, landing our Artillery and Stores, and providing fascines and pickets for carrying on the *operations* of the Siege. Colonel Burton, Colonel Fraser (just recovered of his wounds), and Colonel Walsh, were appointed to act as Brigadiers.

SEPTEMBER 16TH.—There was a redoubt began at night about four hundred yards from the Works, to cover a Battery to be erected against the Bastion of Sainte Ursule.

SEPTEMBER 17TH.—*There were Proposals sent out in the afternoon for* a CAPITULATION ; and the weather being very wet, *there were no works carried on* that night. The army at Beauport had now almost totally disappeared, which they effected by *stolen* marches from night to night, *and got* up the country by the way of "Lorette," but left a strong guard in the Tête-de-Pont of Saint Charles, to prevent our *pursuing* them by that way. They left the *greater part* of their Tents standing, all their artillery along that coast, and a considerable quantity of Provisions, which was plundered and carried off by the inhabitants.

E

SEPTEMBER 18TH.—In the morning the Capitulation agreed upon was drawn up and signed. The following is a translation of it from the French *language*:

The Capitulation demanded upon the other side has been granted by His Excellency General Townshend, Brigadier of His Britannic Majesty's Forces, in the manner and upon the conditions hereafter express'd:

Articles of Capitulation demanded by Monsieur de Ramzay, The King's Lieutenant, Commanding the High and Lower Town of Quebec, Knight of the Royal and Military Order of Saint Louis, &ca., &ca.; from His Excellency The General of His Britannic Majesty's Troops:

ARTICLE 1ST.

The Garrison of the Town, consisting of the Troops of France, Marines and Sailors, shall go out with Arms, Baggage, Drums beating, Lighted Match, with two pieces of Brass cannon and twelve rounds for each, and shall be embarked as commodiously as possible for the nearest Port in France.

ARTICLE 1ST.

Monsieur De Ramzay demands that his Garrison shall have the honors of War, and be safely conducted to the Army by the shortest road, with Arms, Baggage, six pieces of Brass Cannon, two mortars or Howitzers, and twelve rounds of Ammunition for each piece.

ARTICLE 2ND.

Granted, upon laying down their arms.

ARTICLE 2ND.

That the inhabitants shall be kept in possession of their Houses, Goods, Effects, and priviledges.

ARTICLE 3RD.

Granted.

ARTICLE 3RD.

That the said inhabitants shall not suffer for having carried Arms in the defence of the Town, since they had been forced to do it, and as the inhabitants of the Colonies of the two Crowns serve as Militia-men in them.

ARTICLE 4TH.

Granted.

ARTICLE 4TH.

That the effects of absent Officers, Inhabitants, shall not be molested.

ARTICLE 5TH.

Granted.

ARTICLE 5TH.

That the said inhabitants shall not be Transported, nor to give up their houses, until a definitive Treaty between His most Catholic Majesty and His Britannic Majesty shall so determine.

ARTICLE 6TH.

Free exercise of the Roman Religion and a Safeguard shall be granted to all *religious* persons, as well as to the Lord Bishop, who may come to exercise the functions of his station, freely and decently, when he shall judge proper, until the possession of Canada shall be decided by His Britannic and His Most Christian Majesty.

ARTICLE 6TH.

That the exercise of the "Catholique, Apostolique et Romaine" Religion shall be kept up; that there shall be safeguards given to the Religious Houses of both sexes, particularly to Monseigneur L'Evêque, who, filled with zeal for the Religion, and with charity for the people of his diocese, and desirous of residing there constantly to exercise freely and with decency his functions, and the misteries of the Roman Religion, and his episcopal Authority in the Town of Quebec when he shall judge proper, until the possession of Canada shall be decided by a Treaty between His most Catholic and Britannic Majesty.

ARTICLE 7TH.

Granted.

ARTICLE 7TH.

That the Artillery and warlike Stores shall be faithfully given up, and inventories of them made out.

ARTICLE 8TH.

Granted.

ARTICLE 8TH.

That the Wounded, Sick, Commissaries, Surgeons, Apothecaries, and other persons employed in the Service of the Hospitals, shall be treated according to the Treaty of Exchange of the 6th February, 1759, agreed upon between Their Most Christian and Britannic Majesties.

ARTICLE 9TH.

Granted.

ARTICLE 9TH.

That previously to giving up the Gate or entrance to the Town to the English Troops, Their General will please to order some soldiers as Safeguards to the Churches, Convents, and principal houses.

ARTICLE 10TH.

Granted.

ARTICLE 10TH.

That the King's Lieutenant Commanding in the Town of Quebec shall be permitted to send to inform the Marquis de Vaudreuil, the Governor-General, of the surrender of the place; also, that he may write to the minister of France to inform him of it.

ARTICLE 11TH.

Granted.

ARTICLE 11TH.

That the present Capitulation shall be executed according to its form and tenor, without being liable to failure under pretence of reprisals, or the non-performance of any preceeding Capitulation.

The present Treaty has been made, and Duplicates kept by us. Signed and Sealed in the Camp before Quebec, the Eighteenth day of September, in the Year one thousand seven hundred and fifty-nine.

CHARLES SAUNDERS.

GEO. TOWNSHEND.

DE RAMZAY.

The same evening we took possession of the Town, with some Companies of Grenadiers, who mounted the Guards, agreed upon to prevent irregularities, and such other Guards as were judged necessary for the Security of the place.

There were two Battalions *marched into* the Town, the Barracks not being in a condition to receive any more for the present.

We found the Buildings in general in a most ruinous condition, *and* infinitely worse than we could have imagined; for, besides those burnt, there was hardly a house in the Town that was not injured by either shot or shells; nor were they habitable without some repairs.

The Fortifications, which consisted only of the fronts towards the Land, were little more than half-finished, and could have held out but a *very* few days after the opening of our batteries; for, there being neither ditch, cover'd-way, nor out-works, the Scarp-wall was exposed to view in many places from the top of the parapet to the foundation. The inside was equally imperfect, and its defense in many places impracticable, even for small arms. There was found in the Town, and along the Coast of Beauport, Two hundred and thirty-four pieces of Cannon, Seventeen Mortars, and four Howitzers, Brass and Iron of all sizes included; six hundred and ninety-four Barrels of Powder; fourteen thousand eight hundred round shot; fifteen hundred shells; three thousand muskets with Bayonets; and seventy tons of musket-shot, with many other articles of less value.

There remained but a small quantity of Provisions, scarcely enough to serve the Garrison for four days, and that was distributed to the Women and children of the poorer inhabitants. The reason of this scarcity was that the French never had above a fortnight's provisions in the garrison at a time, from the fear of their being destroyed by our red-hot shot or shells: they were, therefore, supplied from above and from the army at Beauport as occasion required. The supplies being so precarious was undoubtedly one of the principal causes of their sudden capitulation, for they had but little hopes of the garrison being regularly fed.

The number *of men* who carried arms in the Town, at the time of the Capitulation, was about two thousand five hundred. Of these, there were about eighteen hundred regulars, marines, and sailors sent to France ; the remainder *continued* in the Country under the terms of the Capitulation. The Enemy's loss in Town, during the Siege, amounted to about one hundred men. Their expense of ammunition must have been inconsiderable, for their fire upon our Batteries at Pointe-*des*-Pères was faint, and their fire upon our Works upon the Hauteur d'Abraham was but of a few days' continuance, which, with the small quantity found in Town, especially of Powder, makes it probable that there *was* no great plenty of ammunication in the country.

Our loss of men and expense of ammunition, during the whole Campaign, stood as follows, vizt.:

	Killed.	Woun'd.	Total.
Officers	18	107	125
Non-Commissioned Officers, Drummers, and Private Men	252	1116	1368
Total............	270	1223	1493

Expense of Ammunition.

Round Shot....	32-pounder......................	18,000
	24 do.	18,350
	12 do.	1,000
	6 do. with wood bottoms....	400
Powder—Barrels of.............................		3,880
Musket-shot—Tons..............................		13
Shells.........	13-inch........................	3,000
	10 do.	2,300
	8 do.	1,000
	5½ and 4⅖	none.

Brigadier-General Monkton, being a good deal recovered of his wounds, resumed the Command. The advanced season of the year, which must oblige our Fleet to depart soon, and the work that must necessarily be done to accommodate and secure ourselves for the ensuing winter, rendered it now impracticable to continue the operations of the campaign any longer. There were so many difficulties to struggle with, that it was thought doubtful by some what measures might be most adviseable to pursue, either to retain the place or to demolish and abandon it. Depositing and securing our Provisions ; Repairing Barracks and Quarters ; Improving and securing our Works against assault and surprise ; Providing a sufficiency of Fuel for the Winter, &ca., &ca., were all of them works of great labor, and almost equally pressing. But the advantages which must arise from *keeping* the place, whether Peace or War ensued, and a confidence in the Troops, who were now thoroughly inured to fatigue and danger, made the doubts upon that head soon vanish. It was, therefore, determined to keep the place at all hazards, and immediate measures were taken accordingly.

There was a Staff appointed, and such works as required the most immediate attention were began upon without delay. Brigadier-General Murray was appointed Governor, and Colonel Burton Lieutenant-Governor; with such other Staff *appointments* as are usual in a British *Garrison*.

Transcribed from rough memoranda, by
JAS. THOMPSON, Junr.
1821.

The foregoing is not in the *usual* mode of my Father's recitation, but is not the less *Authentic*.

French Force.   *Men.*

The Quebec Brigade, commanded by Colonel De Saint
   Ours, on the right................................... 3,500
The Brigade of Three Rivers, commanded by Monsr.
   De Borme, on the right........................ 900
The Centre, to be composed of regular Troops, com-
   manded by De Sénézergues.................... 2,000
The Montreal Militia, on the left, commanded by
   Monsr. Prudhomme 1,100
The Brigade of the Island of Montreal, Commanded by
   Monsr. Herbin................................ 2,300
The Cavalry, chiefly regulars...................... 350
Light Troops, chiefly Canadians and Acadians....... 1,400
Indians, exclusive of the Scouting and Scalping parties. 450
                                                   ————
                                                  12,000

   This force was ranged, in order of Battle, from the Bridge
of the River St. Charles to the Falls of Montmorenci, to
oppose the landing of the British in that quarter.

   The Garrison of Quebec was defended by the Militia and
a few regulars, under the Command of DeRamzay.

   The Battle was more remarkable for display of courage
than for Scientific manœuvre, and was chiefly decided by the
Bayonet and Broadsword, the agile Highlanders serving,
in a manner, to supply the want of Cavalry, while the
steadiness of the English Fuziliers rendered the want of
Artillery less felt. General Wolfe bestowed his whole
attention upon the steady advance of his Right Division
(right to the St. Lawrence), injudiciously exposing himself
in the front of the line. He was repeatedly wounded, (one
of the wounds being through the wrist of the Sword-arm,)
and at length mortally, at the moment the French were giving
way, and were pursued by the Highlanders, who, for the
purpose of their indulging in their national mode of attack

with the less constraint, had thrown away their fuzees; and the Broadsword soon told a dreadful account of the Slaughter that took place, on the view taken of the ground after the confusion of the retreat had somewhat subsided. The *pursuit* of the Highlanders was across the slope, in a direction towards the General Hospital ; but a great part of the *retreat* was through the Town, by St. John's and St. Lewis Gates, and out again through Palace Gate, along the Beach, towards the Ferry at St. Charles River.

My Father held no Rank in the Army, but Volunteered his Services in order to accompany a particular Friend, Captain Baillie, who obtained a Company in Fraser's Highlanders, which Regiment was raised in the Town of Tain, Ross-shire, in four days, and numbered upwards of fourteen hundred men, Commanded by Colonel Simon Fraser. On the passage to Halifax, Captain Bailey introduced my Father to the Colonel, who promised to use his interest in procuring for him a Commission ; but no vacancy having occurred, and the Regiment having been disbanded after the Conquest of Louisbourg, Quebec and Montreal, he was left without employment. At length, in 1761, he was offered the situation of Barrackmaster of Quebec, or Town-Major of Montreal ; but, being by Profession an Engineer, he chose the Appointment of Superintendent of Military Works, which was conferred upon him by General Murray, and which he held until his decease in 1830—69 years, corresponding with the number of years that I have been a member of the Commissariat, having joined on the 15th October, 1798. My Father died at Quebec in his 99th year.

The foregoing Memo. Noted in January, 1867.

JAS. THOMPSON,
D. C. Gl.

NOTE.

CERTAIN persons, strangers to Canada and its people, and very little conversant with its history, having, in the course of the controversy referred to in the first note, endeavored to throw doubt on the respectability, standing in society, and competency to write of the late James Thompson, senr., and having hinted more than doubts of the veracity of both himself and son, I have thought it well to annex a few documents bearing on the subject, written by contemporaries, some of whom still live. I shall, however, in the first place, premise some facts connected with his family and self:—Mr. Thompson's parents were in that position of life which enabled them to give all their children an excellent education for that day. His eldest brother, William, was Adjutant of the 1st or Royal Scots, from whence he exchanged to the 41st, and after active service abroad returned to England, and resided at Berwick-on-Tweed, in the enjoyment of retired full-pay, till his death. Mr. Jas. Thompson, junr., having given a statement in connection with his father, it is unnecessary to repeat it.

[No. 1.]

" This is to certify that the bearer hereof, Mr. James Thompson, having been employed as OVERSEER OF WORKS in the Engineer Department of this place since the year 1772, has been recommended to me, by the officers under whom he served, for his attention and fidelity, &c.; and having discharged his duty to my satisfaction, during my command, and being *an old and faithful servant of the Crown*, I have thought fit to continue him in his present employment, and do hereby recommend him to the favour and protection of all officers who may hereafter succeed to this command.

" Given under my hand, at Quebec, this 8th November, 1784.

"(Signed,)   "FRED. HALDIMAND."

[No. 2.]

" By General His R. H. Edward, Duke of Kent, &c., &c.

" It having been judged expedient, for the better regulation of the
[L.S.]   works carried on in the Garrison of Quebec, in the contingent line,
under the direction of the Chief Engineer, that an *Overseer* should be appointed to *superintend* the artificers and labourers employed in the Department of the officer above named, you are hereby empowered and directed to take upon yourself the several duties attached to such situation, and to hold yourself responsible for the attention, good guidance, and

regularity of those placed under your immediate controul, carefully observing to obey such instructions as you may from time to time receive through the General Orders, and from the chief or subaltern Engineer ; and as a proper encouragement for your exertions in the zealous discharge of this duty, you will be entitled to receive *the daily pay of seven shillings and sixpence, Halifax currency, together with the several allowances of lodging and fuel,* which, by the general schedule, are attached to the situation of an *Overseer of the Works, established as such by warrant from England or from the Commander-in-Chief.*

"Given under my hand and seal, at head-quarters, Halifax, this 22nd day of October, 1799.

"(Signed,)   "EDWARD.

"By order of H. R. H. the Commander-in-Chief,

"(Signed,)   "JAMES WILLOUGHBY GORDON,
"Military Secretary.

"To James Thompson, Esq., Overseer to the Works, Quebec."

[No. 3.]

"HEAD-QUARTERS, HALIFAX, June 21, 1800.

"Sir,—I am honored with the commands of H. R. H. the Duke of Kent to acknowledge your letter of 28th ulto., which was received here *yesterday.* His R. H. *is well convinced of your meritorious and long services;* and being always desirous of extending his patronage to those who appear to be deserving of it, he has, in the present instance, *actually anticipated your request,* and your warrant was transmitted by me in a letter to Lieut.-Gen. Hunter of 7th April last, and which it is to be hoped will before this period have been safely deposited in your possession.

"I have the honor to be, sir, &c., &c.,

"JAMES WILLOUGHBY GORDON,
"Military and Private Secretary.

"To James Thompson, Esq., Overseer to the Works, Quebec."

[No. 4.]

"Dear Sir,—I think I have seen lately in town your son, who has been stationed at the Cedars. Will you do me the favour to accept a quiet dinner with me next week?—I will say Wednesday;—and I ask the favour, particularly, that you would bring with you all your sons now with you. I can only assure them they never can find an introduction that I should esteem more highly.

"Yours,　"DALHOUSIE.

"Castle of St. Louis, Friday.

"Mr. Thompson, Overseer of Works, Engineer Depart., Quebec."

[No. 5.]

"Dear Sir,—Will you do Lady. Dalhousie and myself the favor to dine with us on Wednesday next? I shall hope to see your three sons with you.

"Yours, with great respect,

"DALHOUSIE.

"Monday morning, 8th Jany., 1827.

"Mr. Thompson, Ordnance Office."

[No. 6.]

"My Dear Sir,—I gave you no answer to your last letter and walk down to the Castle; and it, therefore, gives me pleasure to do, without any solicitation, that which I hope will assure you of my wish to testify my respect for you and yours. I have this moment named your son to be Judge in Gaspé, an important and respectable station in society, and which must grow more in consequence as society increases and enlarges in that fine district of Canada.

"Yours most truly,

"DALHOUSIE.

"21st March, 1827.

"Mr. Thompson, Senr., Engineer Office."

N. B.—The above letters from Lord Dalhousie are selected from many similar.

[No. 7.]

On his death, in 1830, Dr. Fisher, so well known and respected by everybody in Quebec, wrote and published:

"From his general intelligence, *particularly on military points*, his strong memory, faculties which enabled him to treasure up a store of most interesting anecdotes, and which, up to a period *nearly approaching his dissolution*, he would freely relate in all their minuteness of circumstances, and with all his frankness of manner, he acquired general esteem, in which he had the happiness to number that of each succeeding Commander of the Forces, and which seems to have gained strength with his increasing years."

[No. 8.]

On the same occasion, Colonel Cockburn, R.A., who served and lived so long in Quebec, and who knew Mr. Thompson well, wrote in his *Quebec and its Environs :*—" This veteran has since paid the debt of nature : he died on Wednesday, 25th Augt., 1830, in the 98th year of his age. Mr. Thompson was for a long period Overseer of Works in the Engineer Department of the Garrison. He was born in Tain, in Scotland, and came to this country in General Wolfe's army, and was at the capture of Louisbourg, and in the sanguinary but unsuccessful affair at Beauport. His memory enabled him at all times to relate many of the adventures of the different engagements which preceded the fall of Quebec. He also took part in the defence of this city against. the attacks of the American Generals, Arnold and Montgomery, in December, 1775. As a soldier he was intrepid ; as a servant of the King he was strictly faithful. To these qualities he added many of the domestic virtues. He reared a numerous family, and his sons are now in situations of trust and honor. On the 27th his remains were conveyed to the grave with military honors, and attended by a numerous concourse of civilians. The band and firing-party were furnished by the 15th Regt., the senior corps in garrison, which, by a singular coincidence, happens to be one of those which formed the army under General Wolfe."

I have been voluntarily furnished by two witnesses, still living, with testimony as follows :

[No. 9.]

Dr. Douglas writes from Glenalla :—" I have read, with great interest and satisfaction, your communications anent old Mr. Thompson ; and, although complete in themselves, I could have verified and added to them from my intimate personal knowledge of the old gentleman during the last four years of his life."

[No. 10.]

Mr. Charles Aylwin writes from *Cap Santé :*—" I have noticed, with some interest, several communications which appeared in the columns of the *Quebec Gazette*, in relation to the ' Expedition against Quebec in 1759.'

Though I have not the pleasure of your acquaintance, you will permit me, with all [respect, to offer some observations in the matter, which may tend to vindicate and establish the truth of what you have asserted in your various communications. I really cannot understand how Mr. Walkem (whoever he may be) can seek to lower the social status, at the period mentioned, of the late Mr. James Thompson, senior ; but this I know, as a truth, that I have a perfect recollection, when a youth at Quebec, of having read, with interest, *the manuscript volumes of the late Mr. James Thompson, senr.*, and I have ever remembrance of them. I also perfectly remember having read in the manuscript volumes which were lent for his perusal to my late father, Thomas Aylwin, the incidents there mentioned and related, and a copy of which I will endeavor to find here. Without the least desire of being obtrusive, you will believe me to be very truly yours."

But the manuscripts in my possession speak for themselves—four folio and four small volumes.

[No. 11.]

The Revd. L'Abbé Casgrain, a member of the Historical Document Committee, to whom the matter was referred, spoke thus in reply to a very lengthy statement of Dr. Miles, the Assistant-Secretary of the Bureau of Public Instruction :

"I hold in my hand the manuscript under discussion.. I knew well Mr. James Thompson, junr. He was an accomplished scholar, and spoke French as purely as I do. I have frequently consulted him in my historical researches, and have made use of the information thus received. At a time when little attention was paid to the preserving and recording the events in Canadian history, both he and his father distinguished themselves by their devotion to it. I have had access to their journals. I know well the writing of Mr. James Thompson, junr.; I recognise it in this journal. I would as soon believe that that sun which is now shining upon us would not rise to-morrow as that he would have attached his signature to this memorandum had he not written this journal from *rough memoranda*. But, irrespective of this, I think the journal of such intrinsic value that I think the Society ought to publish it just as we have got it."

[No. 12.]

"Brompton Barracks, Chatham, April 27, 1872.

"My Dear Dr. Anderson,—I shall willingly give you all the information in my power regarding the authorship of the account of the expedition to Quebec in 1759.

" The R. E. Corps papers of 1849 (which are now on my table) contain 'A short account of the expedition against Quebec, commanded by Major-General Wolfe, in the year 1759, by an engineer on that expedition (Major Moncrief), communicated by Col. G. G. Lewis, C.B., R.E.'

" The above is a true copy of the table of contents of the volume, as far as it applies to the article in question.

"In the year 1856 or 1857, when I was Brigade-Major of Engineers, or, more properly, Assistant-Com. R. Engineers, I instructed Mr. Pilkington, who was then the senior Surveyor and Draftsman in the office of the Com. R. Engineers in Canada, to make a copy of the article in question, as well as of the plan attached to it. This copy was prepared for the information of General Sir W. Eyre, K.C.B., then commanding in Canada, and *afterwards returned by him to the Commanding R. Engineer.*

"Mr. Walker, Surveyor and Draftsman, from his official position, *had access to this document,* and has communicated it (I presume with Colonel Hamilton's permission) to the public press.

" When I visit London again I shall consult the army-lists of that period, and ascertain *whether Major Moncrief was an Engineer officer.*

"It is just possible that the initials P. M., at the end of the paper, are those of Major Peter McKellar, who attached his initials in order to stamp Major Moncrief's official account with the authority of the Commanding Engineer of the army.

" *I fear I cannot ascertain from whom the late Gen. Lewis received the paper.*

" Giving you permission to make any use you please of this note, believe me, my dear Doctor Anderson, yours very truly,

" T. L. GALLWEY,
" Colonel R. Engineers.

" Dr. Anderson, President Lit. and Hist. Society, Quebec."

www.ingramcontent.com/pod-product-compliance
Lightning Source LLC
Chambersburg PA
CBHW031818090426

42739CB00008B/1334